A Leaf between my Toes

Finding Wonder

Jane Upchurch

To Josie
with love
from
Jane 3/13

A Leaf between my Toes

Onwards and Upwards Publishers

Berkeley House, 11 Nightingale Crescent, Leatherhead, Surrey, KT24 6PD.

www.onwardsandupwards.org

The opinions represented in this book are the author's own and do not necessarily reflect the position and views of the publisher, its employees and associates.

About the Author

Jane's writing links a love of this planet, its rocks and oceans, trees and bees, with awareness of the intimacy and wildness of God. It is a way of growing closer to the things she writes about; it is a way of growing in love.

Her journey has included living in community at the Findhorn Foundation, celebrating Jewish festivals with her family and hosting a church in her home. Her writing bridges Christian and holistic spirituality. She particularly likes the concept in Celtic spirituality of creation as a self-giving of God.

She has qualifications in biology, geology and theology as well as counselling, education and pastoral studies. She has worked with young people, the unemployed and people with a mental health or substance abuse problem. She home-schooled her daughters when they were young.

Jane is a spiritual companion; she takes services in a local church and runs groups in the community including a meditation group. She is a member of a dance company and loves Cole Porter, crime novels and colour. She lives on the Western edge of London with her husband Bill, her daughters Joy and Grace and her dog Jenny.

www.janeupchurch.co.uk

A Leaf between my Toes

Introduction

Wonder is a discovery that lifts a dull day.

It surprises us, taking the cover off our ordinary existence to show the life, the effervescence, that was hidden before. It is a window through the mundane into another world which we realise is our own world come anew and we are welcome there.

Wonder gifts us back our life, our situation, our surroundings, with generosity. It enlarges our hearts so they fill with the qualities we honour. It is part of love and of gratitude; it is a link with what is sacred; it is a way of worship.

If we take time to notice, to listen, to wonder, we are called out of ourselves. It can happen as we drive to work or sit quietly at home. It can happen on holiday or as we walk the dog. It can happen in our garden.

I have made a gravel sanctuary in a hidden space at the bottom of my garden. There are laurel and elder bushes behind and hawthorn overhead. I have two seats, both with room for me and my dog. One faces up the garden, through the screen of the rose trellis, past the apple and plum trees to a little grove of birch in the middle. The other faces east so I can watch the rising sun. In the middle is a water feature that trickles over stone. I come down here each morning, twenty minutes to sit, to read or write or think, to feel part of the natural world, to wonder. Join me.

> *"For the Celtic Imagination ... experience ... was an event of revelation; ... the mind always had at least one window facing the eternal. Through this window wonder and beauty could shine in on a life and illuminate the quiet corners where mystery might be glimpsed."*[1]

---

[1] *From Divine Beauty: The Invisible Embrace by John O'Donohue, published by Bantam Press. Used by permission of The Random House Group Limited. Copyright (c) 2004 John O'Donohue. Reprinted by permission of HarperCollins Publishers.*

Spring is Beginning to Show

Spring is beginning to show.
The warming sun
and early flowers
perfume the air that I breathe.

I have waited so long for this.

My body carries
the sluggishness of winter,
my mind is dulled,
my spirit lethargic.

I will breathe the spring
into my lungs,
into my blood, into my cells.

I will let the life
of the spirit of spring,
the spirit of God,
quicken me.

I breathe in spring,
I breathe out winter.

I breathe in spring,
I breathe out winter.

I will rest, anchored to the earth,
trusting that new growth
will green me,
new sun will warm me,
new life will enliven me.

I am part of this process.

Breathing in spring

Jane Upchurch

The End of Dawn

The sun
rolls into the waiting sky
as the earth tilts towards it.

Birds sing in attendance,
the air quickens like an ocean
ready to move.

I sit at the end of dawn,
at the edge of the garden,
matching my strength to its pull,
playing the day
through shoals of unmarked time.

Playing the day

Spring Sings

Spring sings its loveliness,
warming the stiffened boughs,
the hardened soil,
the sleepy souls.
Bees are humming a hymn,
birds are fluting the skies,
the sun is soothing my skin.

The green of the grass
glows yellow
with the pleasure of it
as does my soul.

This is my worship today,
a full-body joining
with the hymn of life
that spring is singing
in my garden.

Worshipping with the spring

Bless the Rain

The air is still inside this room,
still and silent
like a door to another world.

Outside, the air hangs with rain,
carrying the chill of the clouds.

Everything is touched by it,
glistening with wet surfaces.

Bless the rain,
bless the egalitarian gift of it
dampening or drenching
everything in its parish.

Bless the cleansing of it,
shining leaves, sharpening the air.
Bless the goodness of it,
nourishing plants
and ultimately us.

Bless the movement of it,
sweeping in from oceans,
then on again with the breeze.

Bless the rain
for being something
we can't control,
for being bigger than us,
waylaying our feet,
reshaping our well-worn paths.

Bless the life of it,
and my life under it.

Bless the rain.

Blessing the rain

Perfume

The mahonia blossom
scents all the air around it
so, lost in thought,
I stop and look
for the source of the perfume
and smile.

May my love
be as perfume,
the things I do
be as incense
so that my love
and my life
may bring you smiles.

Perfuming the air

Jane Upchurch

Humble Hands

Walking or driving along
the same roads each morning,
passing the same trees,
shows the unfolding of spring.

Branches start bare
then bit by bit
they burst into green.

The Norwegian maple
starts with flowers,
not pretty blossom
but yellow-green,
bright tufts on brown branches
that light the lanes,
growing daily into
a shower of stalks and flowers.

The horse chestnut is bolder,
big brown sticky buds burst
into arching green fingers,
erupting bottom first
like a breech birth
then opening like an umbrella
to catch the sun
with huge hands.

I too will open today,
will unfold my limbs and my heart
to the sun,
to the spirit of spring,
to the spirit of God,
holding their light and love
with humble hands.

Unfolding with spring

Jenny

Each morning
when I sit to begin in stillness
my dog is next to my thigh,
checking out the breeze,
sharing the moment.

She is always aware of where I am
and loves to be with me.

She makes my day.

Can I make God's day?

Making God's day

Jane Upchurch

At the Bottom of my Garden

I am at the bottom of my garden
facing East,
the sun bright on my face,
on my lids.

The birdsong makes a bower
wherever I sit.
The distant hum of traffic
confirms this place
as an oasis, as sacred space.

The privilege of rising early
is being greeted by the rising sun,
the new-born day.

Prayer is sitting open to this place,
to the sun,
to the sound of birds,
to the newness about to begin.

Prayer is letting my heart
be filled with this peace
as preparation for the day.

Letting my heart be filled

Surprises

My garden is not trim and tidy. It is tended and loved, but wild around the edges. It catches seeds from the air and grows them into plants or trees so there are almost as many wild flowers here as in the local Nature Reserve. Some are a nuisance, but others are a delight, especially as they are a surprise, a gift. My favourite are the violets, deep green heart-leaves with purple faces above.

Blow on me, wind of the spirit. Plant surprises in my soul that will grow to feed my need for beauty and bring delight to others. Fill my bare patches, green me where I'm brown.

Show me the things I thought were weeds that are really wild flowers so I might love myself more as you do. Unlock my lips, my heart, my hands so the seeds I grow can be scattered, carried on your wind to find the bare soil in the people I live among.

Tend my garden with me. Help me to trust your wildness.

Scattering seeds

Birch Leaf

Little green leaves, welcome. Welcome to my garden, to the spring, to this world. You are so small and new, almost transparent, shining with the afterglow of birth. Some of you are the size of a baby's fingernail, some of you are the size of mine.

What is it like, being poured into the air, breathing it in and out to fire your green cells? What is it like, loving the sun so much that you hold your face to catch it? What is it like dancing in the breeze, free to float yet held by your branch, by your body? Do you feel a communion with the other leaves, with the trunk, with the roots? Does the sap you drink bring you their stories?

You are so perfect for what you do, getting on with it quietly, living the life of a little green leaf in its fullness. I will trust that I too am perfect for what I have to do.

Spending time with a tree

Random

Thank you for this glorious day. The sun is sailing the calm blue sky with hardly a breeze to blow its sails. The birds are adorning the trees with song. The oak looks like it has been daubed with dangling moss as it flexes its baby leaves and catkins. And there are flowers.

Thank you for the tulips, an almost white yellow with chalices instead of cups and sceptres at their centre. Thank you for the plum blossom, white and busy with bees, preparing for a future harvest. Thank you for the kerea, orange furry balls like little suns. And thank you for the carpet under the fruit trees, primroses yellow and pink, cow skips tall and nodding, scattered amongst the forget-me-nots.

Its loveliness is partly its randomness, growing where thrown by the wind. Thank you for all the random events in my life, the people I am thrown against, the situations that grip me that are none of my choosing. Thank you for bursts of beauty I didn't expect.

Being grateful

To Be Here

The important thing
is to be here.

The important thing
isn't to write,
or to think profound thoughts,
or compose words of prayer

but to touch the sand
with my hand,
to feel the soft salt
of the sea breeze on my skin

and to breathe,
just to breathe
the air.

Being here

Holiday

Here I am on holiday
with the smell of freshly baked rolls
permeating the kitchen,
the sounds of people I love talking,
moving, sneezing,
and others I love
filling the house
with the weight of their sleeping.

The sun is shining
and there is a blue sky
to move into
promising more,
promising a proper holiday day.

Today my worship
will be the love of friends,
the change of scene,
my favourite beach
and the glory of the sun.

Worshipping where I am

Skin

What a gift to be clothed in skin,
not hidden by fur or feathers
or rigid in a stiff casing.

My skin can breathe,
can feel the air moving upon it.
It glows with the sun
and chills with the passing cloud,
pulling all its little hairs tall
to hold a blanket of air around me.

If I hold my arm at eye level
I can see them,
my almost invisible friends.

I love the smell of my skin
when it's been in the sun.
My skin isn't inert; it responds,
releasing its own perfume for
sunny days.

My skin is my interface
with the world,
made so I can feel,
so I can sense its seasons,
so I can be part of it.

My skin moves around me
whatever shape I take,
whatever I choose to do.

My skin holds me in,
it defines me.
It ages with me
so neither of us are so tight,
weathering the ways of the world
with grace.

Loving myself

A Meditation

Driving from Dorset
to Cornwall,
following the flow of the road
through hedgerows
of new green buds
and woods that invite you in,
the sun singing overhead,

the verges thick with dandelions,
egg-yolk yellow and rich,
daisies scattered like confetti,

clusters of lemon-yellow primroses
or wild, white flowers,

skylines of black-branched trees,
sheep in the meadow,
and so many greens,

here the blackthorn
in white flower,
there the yellow of gorse,

the sky filling more than
half the view
leading us on,
clouds playing with the blue.

Revelling in the view

Days Aren't Always Sunny

Days aren't always sunny.
Grey skies and chilled air
match my mood.
I have problems I cannot solve,
pain and fears I cannot fix.

Sitting here is a comfort,
a wild place floored with fallen
leaves
like last year's hopes,
brown and curled and finished.

Ivy pushes through them
and brambles are starting
their green surge
under the mossy branches,
beneath the dead tree.

Not the kind of life
I would have chosen.

There is a stream running through,
cold, clear water
burbling as it runs over rocks,
the sound staying here
while the stream moves on.

I take my troubles
and lay them in the stream.

I take my pain
and lay it in the leaves.

I take my sorrow and confusion
and dig it into the muddy ground.

Laying my pain down

Buddleia

There is a buddleia
next to the stream,
huge and wild,
the new spring leaves scattered
among the tangle of branches
and last year's blooms,
a web of living and dead.

My buddleia at home
is like a different beast,
all pruned ready for a new season.

Is this part of what scares us
about the wild,
the acceptance and inclusion of
death?

I have pruned
many things from my past
but underneath the surface
I still carry last year's growth.

It weights me,
it is a frame for my future.

There is more of the wild about me
than I let on,

the tangle of my inner self,

the death I can carry,

the life that goes on growing.

Accepting the wild

Jane Upchurch

Primroses

The old stone wall
has become part of the land.
Moss and grass,
ferns and wild flowers,
cover it in haphazard beauty.

There is a bank
of primroses,
soft green leaves
like rabbits ears
and tumbling masses of yellow.
I will paint them with words
so I can revisit them
when far away.

The flowers are flat
on thin, pink-tinged stalks,
five bi-lobed petals
like pale, long hearts,
all joined as one
at the base,
at the saffron-coloured centre.

There is such a
small, round opening
filled with the green orb
of the stigma
or the clustered yellow filaments
of the anthers,
pin-eyed or thrum-eyed,
complimenting each other
when the insects visit.

They look like bouquets
waiting for the spring fair.

They hallow their surround,
shining among
the green of the bank.

Remembering the flowers

Silence

Silence.
Opening up
to the living space
that was hidden
below the noise.

Letting myself rest
in the here
and now.

Nothing to do,
no-where to go
but this.

Dropping through the emptiness
into the fullness
of silence.

Sitting
in the company of angels,
in the company of God,
in the company of my soul.

Sitting in silence

Replace the Chaos

I've been away.
Come, garden,
and bring me back to you.
Ground me in your earthiness
and fill me with your peace.
Settle me again
in who I am
and where I am going.
I've lost my roots.

If I sit here, just sit here,
I can let them grow again.
I can let this oasis
of natural life
replace the chaos
that I feel.

This is my home.
If I sit here I can find
my rightful place again.

Just sitting

Blossom

My garden
is my sanctuary.
I can sit here
with my troubles
and let them leak
into the ground.

The birds are singing,
the flowers are blooming,
the air is inviting.
They are not worried.

Next to me is a blossom tree
covered with deep pink flowers.
They are new and beautiful.

I am going to plant them inside me
so they will perfume
my day.

Letting my troubles go

Jane Upchurch

The Magic of Forgiveness

What a cluster of bothers
I gather,
letting the negative
stick to me
like hooked seeds
and the wonder and joy
slip past like melted butter.

I will unhook them
with the magic of forgiveness.
I list each person,
each event,
and as I say the words
the seeds tumble away
with my breath.

I forgive.

Forgiving each one

Day and Night

Driving west
the sun hangs low
ahead of me
like a friendly face,
beaming red,
so I find myself
beaming back
and shaking
with the laughter
of joy.

Returning home
the moon is now ahead
hanging low and full,
shining mellow
with a different kind of blessing.

Day and night
we are watched over,
we are enlightened,
we are blessed.

Beaming at the sun

Oak

The oak tree is out.
There are dangly brown catkins
and leaves yellow-green and small.
They haven't swelled
to fill the whole tree yet,
they are verdant islands
in a sea of blue sky.

The oak tree is master
of our gardens,
sitting at the corner of four
so none of us are overcome
by his size.
His is a quiet authority,
a presence that guards the garden
whether in full leaf or bare.

I owe him my respect,
I venerate his shelter.

Venerating the oak

Spring

I could fill a whole book
with spring.
Everywhere I look
life is bursting out,
such flowers, such scents,
and new-born leaves
so delicate and perfect.

I cheer as I see them,
stopping to look, to touch,
to smell.

Beauty calls forth beauty
and I blossom with them,
both of us offering
a hymn of praise
with our smiles.

Responding to spring

Mirrors

Sitting on the swing seat
caught in this moment of day,
feeling the breath of it
on my neck,
adorned with sun,
full as a pea pod.

I can hear the silence,
nearer than the birdsong,
than the distant rumbles of people.

The birch leaves shine
as they catch the light
like a tree full of mirrors.

Catching the light

Longing

Longing
for my garden.
Longing
for the outside air.

Longing
for the sunshine and new leaves and daisies.
Longing
for sanctuary.

Longing
for quiet.
Longing
to sit in the wash of the spirit of God.

Longing
for peace.

Longing for God

Jane Upchurch

The Ground is a Bed

The ground is a bed
for me to lie on,
the clay accepting my clay
back to itself,
the grass bearing my weight.

My charge is earthed,
my tension collected
by my earth mother.

I lose myself
as I gaze
at the sky.

I lie on my front
in surrender,
smelling the sweetness of grass
and kissing it.

Lying on the earth

May

Welcome May.

Welcome month
at the beginning of the long summer,
of Beltane.

Welcome month
of completeness, of full leaf.

Welcome month
of light, of hope.

I will sing you a song of welcome.

Welcoming with a song

Horse Chestnut Trees

There is a parade
of horse chestnut trees near here,
all now fully clothed,
stately with sculpted leaves
and alight with candles,
some white flowers,
some red.

They are magnificent.

I blow them kisses as I pass.

Blowing kisses to the trees

The Gravel Garden

There is a wind that has been lurking all day, enticing trees to dance, cooling the air, although the sun is still with us in its mid-spring majesty. My water feature has been reborn, now above the ground in a barrel full of pebbles so blind feet can't break it. It bubbles quietly here in my gravel garden, maintaining its gentle pouring while the winds make music with the leaves and the squirrel barks a warning. Only a little sunlight filters in now the leaves are full, dappling the stones in moving patterns. The ferns guard one side, and the laurel and ivy the other, a sanctuary where thoughts can roam or rest.

There are flowers around me too, all white. The laurel has finished, but the hawthorn bower over my head is covered with clusters of white. When they finish the rambling rose buds will open.

The squirrel has gone and a robin is singing. The garden is full of its own music, washing me clean of stale thoughts. It is a place alive this morning.

Listening to the garden

Peony

I can sip beauty,
I can take it up
by osmosis
until it becomes
the lining of my soul,
jewels in the dark.

The peony is lush,
a ball of velvet,
carmine petals
folded together
like pleats
of a heart.

Sipping beauty

Shining

The lime tree shines.
Its flat plates of leaves
overlap each other
like soft armour,
all facing the light
together.

I can align my heart
to shine,
to face the light
and reflect it back
like worship.

Aligning my heart to shine

Another Day

Another day.
Grey skies this morning
so the garden is muted,
no play of light and shade.
It is a green world.

It will be easier to work inside
without the sun
calling me out to play.

I have choices
I can make with my time
today.

It all starts here,
in the quiet,
with the gift
of a new day.

Grateful for the day

Blessing

The blessing
of being alive.
The blessing of green leaves
in their coolness.

The blessing of buttercups
in their joy.
The blessing of sparkling water
and flower-filled air.

The blessing of bodies
that are made for here.
The blessing of God
in all this fullness.

Being blessed

Jane Upchurch

Soaking in the Rain

The earth
has soaked in rain
after weeks of dry weather.

It has come alive,
plumped like the leaves
that had been drooping.

It feels content,
restored to its right way
of being.

It feels grateful.

Restored to our right way of being

Walking my Dog

Walking my dog
five minutes from here
through a strip of green
either side of a spindling river.

Cow parsley and willows edge one side
while brambles tumble
through nettles and dock
the other.

Here are blackthorn and buttercups,
daisies and dandelions,
wild roses and clover,
willow herb and feather grass,
oak and ash and birdsong
with a strip of mown grass
inviting feet and hearts
down the middle.

The natural world
doesn't need a huge canvas
to show its colours.
The spirit of God
doesn't need mountains and majesty
to come out and play.

Finding the green, noticing the spirit

Refuge

Sitting here
the sun filters through
the green leaves
and shines
on my face.

This is a place
of refuge
shielded by trees
where the sun
still comes.

I am sheltered,
I am found.

Letting the sun find me

Into the Garden

What is it
that calls me into the garden
on a soft spring day?

What music
of leaf and space and sun
moves me,
finding harmonies of soul?

The air is charged
with the presence of God
making every garden
an altar
where the mundane and the sacred
meet.

Finding alters

Bruised

I have been bruised
by encounters
with the world of people
and with my response.

Here, here is my home,
here in the cool air
where the ground is firm
under my feet
and the birds sing,

here where the trees
draw earth and sun
into their leaves,
where time is full but slow
and I can breathe in and out
my belonging.

Belonging here

Blackberries

Cooking blackberries
in my porridge;
they leak their taste and colour
leaving a bright carmine streak
as I stir.

Dogs can pick up a scent
that is dilute,
they know what was here.

As I walk this earth
I leave myself behind,
I am part of its flavour.

Choosing the flavour that I leave

Help

Thank you sunshine
for being here gentle
to soothe my soul.

I can get so bothered,
emotions upset,
responsibilities too high,
troubles crowding.

I need God's help here.

I have had my rant
and now I'm going to try
to listen
and to trust.

Help me.

Letting God help me

Windy

The sun is flirting today, covering itself with wind-swept clouds then shining brightly for a moment. The trees too play games of resting, then hurling themselves about as they catch the wind in their leaves. You can hear it coming, moving through the oak tree like an ocean surging, like waves roaring up the beach. Whatever weather visits us today will be blown along like a boat in a storm.

The roses are sheltered, just nodding in the morning air, bequeathing their perfume. Where will it end up? Will someone two streets away suddenly smell its sweetness like unbidden love or will it be lost in the tide?

Hearing the wind

Dorset

Sitting in the sun,
Bill asleep in the campervan,
Jenny next to me on a chair,
the grass dry under my feet,
the blue sky full of singing birds.

Dry limestone walls cross the fields
like old bones.
New stones glow golden,
old stones turn grey,
weathered and patched with lichen,
matching the sheep they are enclosing.

Over their heads
the sea seems to nestle
between the hills,
calling out clouds
from the heavy land.

Finding time to relax

Sitting

I am sitting on the sand,
I am sitting on my planet.

I am rooted in this time,
I am present in this place.

This is my arena for life,
I leave footprints on its face.

Sitting on my planet

An Ordinary Life

This is not an ordinary life.
This is the greatest gift of all.
I will value it before I lose it,
before my limbs or my mind seize.

I will remember the beauty
that went into my making,
the love that holds my heart
so I can come in and go out
in peace.

My life
is an altar
where God and the ordinary meet.

Meeting God in the ordinary

Roses

My bower is strung
with roses,
perfumed pink hanging heavy
and tiny white clusters
opening from yellow fists.

As they fade
the white roses flush pink
and the pink pale to white
as if absorbing each other.

I appreciate
the simple and the showy,
I love their variety,
their colour and perfume.

I am grateful
for passing gifts
that make my day.

Appreciating difference

Obligations

Sometimes I sit here
weighted with obligations.

But they are not me.

The cool greens,
the running water,
the quiet grass
remind me
that I am not defined
by the load I carry,
the busyness, the anxiety,
the pressure.

I am part of the living kingdom,
I am body of the spirit of peace.

Reminding myself

Perfection

My garden is an antidote to perfectionism. For every blade that is trimmed, and dead flower or branch that is cut, there are a myriad others, an ever-changing interplay of life and death, of growth and decay, of beauty and chaos.

But perhaps all is beauty. Perhaps the God who said, 'Be perfect as I am perfect,' meant to prise us away from our tightly wound, hidebound ways into a bigger beauty. Perhaps God's perfection isn't that of a smooth rose but includes the gritty soil, the falling away to fruit and fade only to flower again in the future. Perhaps it isn't the perfection of virtuous lives but of full lives wrapped in the love and learning of God, of letting what feels damaging fall away that it may fade and rot to feed our future.

Perhaps I don't have to be so hard on myself, don't have to try to measure up, but can trust that if I grow my inner garden it will be a place for the spirit of God to walk.

Trusting

The Chaos and the Splendour

There is so much to do
in the garden,
there is so much to do
in the house.

But this is it.
This moment is as full
as it would be
if all were done.

I don't need to chase completion
to feel at peace,
I don't need to aim for perfection
to relax and enjoy.

This is life,
the chaos and the splendour.

Today I will enjoy
the unfinished in my garden
and in me –
my membership card
for this life.

Enjoying the unfinished

Lawns

I don't envy
lawns with stripes.

I like mine full
of flowers
growing up again
each time I mow.

The buttercup and hawkbit
are tall and yellow,
the daisies are short and white,
and hidden in the grass
are self-heal and clover
and the cushioning of moss.

My lawn isn't just grass,
it is ecosystem,
it is community.

Liking

Five Course Meal

Walking down the road,
smelling the flowers
that I pass –
white roses, pink roses,
privet,
mock orange blossom
and honeysuckle,

a five course meal.

Smelling the flowers

My Rule

Religious orders
have a rule they follow,
set ways to love and serve God.

My rule
is my daily life
and my time out most mornings.

Today it is raining
and I am inside.
The room
holds a quality of peace.

I will let it fill my limbs,
I will breathe it slowly
into my tightness.

I will be aware,
listening with my body.

Breathing in peace

Scars

We all carry scars
nestled beside the beauty.

Mine are mainly inside,
messages from my past,
my stamp of belonging
to this world.

Jesus came
with flesh and blood body
and beautiful spirit.

The scars he carries
show he is one of us
and we are part
of him.

Acknowledging our scars

Prayer

Prayer
is for today,
opening to the bowl
of the present,
to the peace
of the spirit of God,
holding in it
ourselves,
our cares,
our day.

Holding the day

Jane Upchurch

Solstice

The longest day of the year
slipped past
shielded by clouded skies.

It didn't feel
like the portent of summer.

Today the clouds
still race
as cool breezes
chase them.

It doesn't look like summer
but I know it is,
a hidden secret
waiting to explode
in hot sunshine
when it is ready.

Anticipating

Summer Sun

The summer sun has come,
oozing its heat
into the heavy air.

In spring,
I seek out the sun
to sit in its pleasure.

Now, I seek out the shade.

I am surrounded by green,
leaves backlit
so they glow yellow-green
and dapple my skin
with their patterns.

I can smell the roses,
I can hear the birds.

All of us are wrapped
in the sun's honey,
languid, softened, open.

Softening

Jane Upchurch

Lichen

My fruit trees
have lichen on their branches,
crusted green-grey
and mustard yellow,
another crop
along with the apples and plums,
telling me
like grey hair
that they have been here
for a while
and are worthy
of my respect.

Respecting

Shelling Peas

Shelling peas.
Every one so perfect,
so round and green and firm
with a little v
where the root would grow
if I planted it.

All so cleverly grown
just for me to eat,
miracles in a mouthful,
life from sun and soil
packed into small green parcels
to feed me.

Eating sunshine

Fullness

This is it,
the fullness has come.

We have climbed the hill
of the lengthening days
and the quickening pulse,
and now we have tipped
over the top
into summer.

All year, the garden
has been preparing for this,
unfurling leaves,
flourishing flowers.

Now it is laid back
in its largesse,
letting the rain fill it,
letting the sun feed it,
offering itself to both
and to us
in all its green majesty.

Offering

My Rock

I have a rock
on my window sill.

It is chalk,
rounded by the sea,
browned by iron
from the sand
and drilled into holes
by molluscs.

As I move around the room
I see a different view
through the opening
scooped at the end
of two twisting tunnels.

One little hole
has its maker lying in it still,
two white shells
hinged together.
What a memorial stone
to have around you.

In my kitchen
I have another world,
part of the sea floor,
caves and caverns
for tiny potholers
to climb through

as I do each time
I look,
caught in the rounded
shapes and hollows
and possibilities.

Seeing another world

Bless You

Bless you sunshine,

Bless you green of trees,
Bless you garden,

Bless you birds,
Bless you running water,

Bless you air,
Bless you stillness,

Bless you God.

Blessing my world

With Arms Out

Walking with arms outstretched
to feel the air,
to open my chest
to the joy of this moment.

Walking with bare feet
to feel the grass
and the solid earth beneath.

Walking with straight back
and happy shoulders
to feel at home in my body,
to trust my place here.

Walking

Blue Geraniums

I have blue geraniums
in a small vase
on my windowsill.
I can see their stigma, style
and stamens,
such delicate, intimate parts.

There are flowers
filling my garden
with their colour, shape
and perfume.

But at all their centres
are the parts that really matter
waiting to spread or gather pollen,
ready to swell and seed,
dropping their pretty petals.

Looking inside

Driving Slowly

Driving slowly
through the rain
I opened the window
a touch
and held my hand
outside,

catching falling drops,
catching water
from the sky,

formed high
above me
and now here
in my hand.

Catching raindrops

Walking the Grass

My garden was so lovely
this morning
but I couldn't linger.

I returned to it
just now
after a shower of rain,
walking the grass
in bare feet,
saying hello
to the new flowers,
removing convolvulus
and dead rose heads
while leaning
into the wet leaves.

I returned to the house
with a leaf between my toes
and a freshness in my heart.

Saying hello

No Words

Sometimes
there are no words.

Just sitting
with the fullness of life,
with the tremor of God.

With the tremor of God

Jane Upchurch

Showers

I love this weather,
sunshine, then heavy rain,
then sunshine again,
glistening on all
the wet surfaces.

It makes me aware
of all the energy out there,
changing and moving
without our direction.

It feels alive.

I am blessed with sun.
I am blessed with rain.

Anything is possible.

Enjoying the weather

The Present

First thing in the morning,
sitting at the bottom of my garden,
ready.

What is this moment for
today?

I shut my eyes
and open it
like a present.

Opening the present

Sunday Morning

It is so peaceful here on a Sunday morning. You can feel the quiet of the street surrounding us, seeping into the garden. The birds are low key, the sun a hazy presence, the leaves gently glowing in their green. This is a time and place to recover from the week's activities. I am going on holiday today so later will be a rush and a pressure, but for now I can just sit here in the balm.

I need this, a sabbath for the soul, sandwiched between my activities. It doesn't have to be for long. I just need to switch off and find a resting place inside. Thank you Sunday.

Nothing to do, nowhere to go

Friends

This is part
of what a friend or partner is for –
someone to get inside my soul
with their love
so that our thorns
and our raw places meet.

How else would we know
where they are,
or why we should trouble
to make amends?

Making amends

Day Prayer

You are never
not here.

I bring my open heart
to this moment,
to the freshness
of this day,
to the presence
of my God.

I can trust you
as I trust the turning night,
as I wake
to dawning light.

Each moment
is an envelope
of your spirit.

I am adrift
on your sea,
I am rooted
in your soil.

My life
is your prayer
for where I am
today.

Bringing my open heart

Tired

I have been travelling.
I have a tired body
and a boggy brain.

The garden
makes no demands of me.

I am allowed
to only be half here.

It is present enough
for the two of us.

Making no demands

Hibiscus

Have you seen
a hibiscus flower?

There are bushes
lining all the paths here,
dark leaves shining
in the heat
and incredible flowers,
rich red or pale pink.

The petals arch back,
pushing their dark centre
towards the sun,
exposing the extravagant length
of a sceptre.
The jewelled head
hangs packets of yellow pollen
below five velvet orbs
of red
wherein lies all its intent.

Noticing something special

Beauty

I come
with my imperfect heart
to the beauty that blazes
from the tired earth

between the dark things,

despite the dark things,

like a redemption.

Finding redemption

The Gift of Spirit

Thank you
for the gift of Spirit
poured out
into this thirsty earth,
drenching roots,
filling flowers and faces,
digging God deep
into the workings
of our planet.

Thank you
for the gift of Spirit
unveiling our eyes,
trembling in our mouths,
in our hearts,
with the awareness
of God as always present,
as secret Santa,
as the hum of life.

Unveiling our eyes

Lizard

A lizard
suddenly appeared
on the flat stones,
in the hot sun.

I thought it was a shadow
until it moved
in short bursts
then paused

like birdsong,

following the shortest path
to the other side.

Seeing hidden things

Selfish

I don't like it
when selfish emotions rear up,
I would want to be peaceful,
calm, neutral.

Not removed from life
but with emotions
that tie me into life,
into the daily round,
with love.

Handling my emotions

The Adaptability of Love

Thank you
that my life is not fixed and sorted and won;
I'm not resting on a plateau of perfection,
however much I think I want to be.

Thank you for the lessons still to learn,
the books to be read,
the people to engage with,
the workings of spirit that still call to me.

Thank you for the cup of my life
and the full mix it contains.

Thank you for the lightness and lure
and adaptability of love,
a golden net swirling, folding
and reconfiguring around every change.

Being grateful for the mix of my life

Jane Upchurch

Getting Up First

There is something special
about getting up first
before the house is awake,
before the noise and routines intrude.

The day is fresh,
newborn,
and so am I.

We take each other's measure.

There are stillnesses to keep.

I have time
to listen to my soul.

Listening to my soul

God of the Garden

God of the garden.

God of the green shoot
and the tall tree.

God of insects and spiders,
God of mould and bacteria
that make it all happen,
God of soil.

God of flowers,
God of colour and scent
and softness,
God of beauty.

God of growth and seasons,
God of pruning and weeding
and dying back.

God of weather.

God of fresh air,
God of stillness and sanctuary,
God of peace.

Seeing God

Hawthorn

The hawthorn leaves and white sky
make patterns like a summer dress.

The branches are rivers and tributaries
flowing through a pale land.

The twigs and leaves make diamonds
like a kaleidoscope.

The top boughs are islands
in a sea of surf.

The world is here.

Making patterns

Sunshine in my Soul

There is sunshine in my garden, there is sunshine in my soul. I have been weeding the latter, throwing out fear and the consequent selfishness and I am like a babe new-born. The morning glistens with possibilities.

Today and all the rest of the week I am seeing friends. Doesn't leave too much time for the other things I need to do but they will grow nicely in the interstices. Behave yourself, fear; I will do it; there will be time. Other days will open for me, and you can't determine my fate today for later. Today all I have to do is what is in front of me – blackberrying, talking, eating, remembering and enjoying. Oh yes!

I've already sent off important emails – YES. I've prepared my talk for Sunday – YES. The sky is blue and singing – YES. Let's gather blessings today and pass them on.

Gathering blessings

Rambling Rose

My rambling rose
has outgrown its trellis.
It is reaching out,
stretching wavering into the air
to hook onto the hawthorn
or apple tree,
to make arches,
to take the splendour
of its pale flowers
into another country.

Reaching out

Sky

It is early evening.
The sky is glazing
from blue to pink to pearl.
There is so much of it.
Ahead there are bars of cloud
striping the sky salmon
and charcoal.
Behind, the clouds
are dim, grey islands
sailing slowly away.
Above they are almost white,
dulling with the falling light.
And moment by moment
it changes.

I can lose myself in it,
allow its space
to find and mirror
space in my soul.
It covers my head,
it is the backdrop to everything.
It always has something to say.

Watching the sky

The Code

This is the code
for approaching a flower
next to the road.

Stop,
draw it towards you gently,
slowly breathe it in,
let it settle in your soul,
kiss its petals,
whisper, 'thank you,'
then move on.

Thanking the flowers

Walking

Walking
is my meditation
today,
putting one foot
in front of the other,
heel to toes,
rhythmic,
connecting with the earth
then letting go,
moving my body
and my awareness
through space,
connecting with this place
then letting go.

Connecting

Jane Upchurch

Rays of Light

The sun
streams through
a crack in the clouds,
rays of light
white against the tousled grey
like a breaking through
of heaven.

Breaking through

Green Glass

A September day
and roses still bloom pink and lush,
hawthorn berries wink red above me
and apples strew the lawn.

The air is cool,
waiting to catch the morning.

As the sun rises
it makes patterns on my lashes,
shining through the green glass
of translucent leaves.

Whatever is imperfect
pales in the balm of it
like muscles easing
under infrared light.

Catching the morning

Jane Upchurch

The Last Day of Summer

Autumn has started
its inroads,
leaves are beginning
to curl and fall,
apples and nuts
have been gathered
and the hedgerows are bright
with berries.

But today I can bask
in the warmth of the sun
feeding my skin,
soaking through to my bones,
topping up my memories
of summer.

Basking in the sun

Evening

Walking the evening streets,
the dusky air
is warm on my face,
the lamps shine gold
silhouetting the trees,
turning green leaves
to burgundy,
bathing the pavement
in welcome.

Bathing in welcome

Jane Upchurch

Moonlight

Today, over the garden,
the moon shone full and round
while the clouds hurried past
without dimming it at all.

It shone so bright
all you could see
in the lens around it
was moon and sky
with the clouds busying themselves
on either side.

Looking at the moon

Smelling Autumn

You can smell autumn
in the air,
the background spice
of browning leaves,
as evocative
as a childhood photo,
as comforting
as toast.

Comforting

Jane Upchurch

Choreography

Lying on the grass,
on my back,
the white clouds above
slowly separate,
the nearer ones
gliding left
while the ones above
sail right,
creating new patterns of blue
with their choreography.

Watching clouds

Gentle

I sit with the sunshine
gentle on my face
breathing in the blessings
of this moment.

I line up my loved ones
in my mind
blowing a blessing
over each of them.

Blowing a blessing

Jane Upchurch

Starlings

Cool blue sky,
late October afternoon,
a scarf of starlings
gathered into a ball
unfolds
as fluid as silk,
sweeps the rooftops
with my heart
flowing with it,
then rolls smoothly away.

Flowing with it

A Call

I can hear a call
on the breeze,
whispering the leaves,
swaying the air
then waiting for a response
like a conversation.

Listening to the breeze

Jane Upchurch

Encounter

The wood
is not so much a place
as a presence,
each tree
holding space
under its branches

like a shelter,
the air along the paths rich
with their slow breath
and the trampled scent
of spice.

The leaves are light,
greens grading to gold
with the sun's flicker,

softening the body
of each vista
like a pulse.

Rain is caught
by the canopy overhead
until it slides earthwards
with plops and drops
long after the rain has stopped.

One falls on my cheek
but I miss
the twirling leaf I chase,
kissing others that still cling
to their branches,
kisses soft as skin.

Kissing the leaves

Twilight in November

The light is fading
out of the air,
out of the garden,
lingering in
the pearly sky
and the white bark.

Twilight in November
and the garden is filled
with the deep peace
of the gathering dark.

Filling with peace

Grey

The morning sky
is grey,
a soft blanket
to the cool air,
to the orange leaves
poured generously
on the grass.

It is a comfort,
a quiet place
of refuge
where any greyness in me
is accepted,
and any fear or sadness
is soothed.

Being accepted

Dusk

The sky is wide,
a wash of colour
filling the far horizon
then vaulting over me
to the horizon behind.
In front
it is apricot and turquoise,
but I can turn my head
and see indigo
ushering in the dusk.

While I walk
the streets darken
as the sun calls back the light
until the trees and houses
are black shapes
and the sky behind glows.

It doesn't take long
for day to turn into evening
and I can be in it,
I can walk through the coalescing air
and see the earth changing
before my eyes.

Seeing the earth changing

Autumn Leaves

The leaves
are putting on a show,
letting their green flow
back to the ground
so they can send the sun
on its way
with glory.

Yellow, gold,
russet and red,
chestnut, magenta,
ochre, terracotta,
sepia and saffron,
all shining bright
then launching themselves
into the air
like confetti.

Glorying in colour

The Sun is a Moon

The sun is a moon
shining white light
through grey cloud.

The trees are dripping
their last leaves
into pools on the ground.

The birds are fast and free,
slaking the thirst
of the air with their wings.

Cars bustle by
in their own shelter,
ignoring or absorbing
the unfolding scene.

Absorbing

Jane Upchurch

Fired with Light

The orange leaves gather
the setting sun
until the trees are fired
with its light.

Gathering the setting sun

Winter Solstice

Winter has crept in,
quietly stripping the last leaves
so that now it is established,
filling the horizon,
come to stay.

The sky is muted shades of grey
like a watercolour wash
behind dark branches
and still firs,
all waiting.

Waiting

Jane Upchurch

Window

The fairy lights hang
on the afternoon sky,
twinkling against the oyster-grey clouds
and the dark firs,
beautifying the landscape,
bringing Christmas
to the cold air.

Beautifying the landscape

Lemon

Cut a thick slice of lemon,

carefully remove the pips
nestled like babies
in the cool flesh.

Hold the slice to the window
and see its segments shine
with their own light,
heavy with juice.

Squeeze and drop it
into a tall, clean, glass
of fresh water

then drink.

Drinking fresh lemon

Jane Upchurch

A Winter's Day

It is dark,
a winter's day.
Inside we have lights
and the cosiness of heating.

Yet looking out,
the garden is not dull and drear
but has its own light

shining in the lawn
as the pale green moss
dapples the grass,

catching the leaves
of the laurel,
reflecting in the water
filling the birdbath,

and blazing from the trunks
of the silver birch
that glow white
like a promise.

Finding light in winter

This Day

This day
woke so beautiful
while I was full of sleep.

The sky softened
into indigo velvet,
bleaching
as it ran to earth,
silhouetting the Scot's Pine,
holding the glow
of the daystar
above it.

Cold had crept in at night
sewing sequins on all the leaves,
ready to glint
in the new-made sun.

As it rose,
the milk-blue sky
filled with scallop shells
of white cloud
like a tropical beach.

Softening like the sky

Jane Upchurch

The Shelter of Dark

Before dawn
in my winter's garden.
It is quiet,

the shelter of dark,
the glow of a light,
birdsong,
Jenny's presence,
me.

I am here.
That is the main gift.
I am here.

Time alone with myself,
with this waiting day,
with my God.

Time alone with myself

Snowlight

It is light in my garden
in the middle of the night,
filled with snow;
the white reflects
the glow of the moon.
It is a place where dreams walk.

Reflecting the glow of the moon

Jane Upchurch

Secret Snow

All day
we waited for the snow
but it came secretly
at night,
falling silently from the dark sky,
blanketing the ground
in stillness,
picking out each twig,
each leaf, each branch,
in white,
in beauty.

Looking at beauty

February

February is an inward month.
I am resting
on the outside
but like the garden
I can sense
shoots and green growths
developing unseen,
promising new things.

Promising new things

Little Things

I have warm slippers
to slip my feet in
as I pad to the dark kitchen.
There is a slice of lemon
in my glug of sparkling water.
The house hums its night song
around me.
The pleasure of little things
is big as a mountain.

Noticing small pleasures

Lavender

I have dripped a drop
of lavender oil
onto my pillow
to help me sleep.

I can breathe in
its gladness,
its stores of sunlight,
its memories of purple flowers
unfolding into
the dark night.

Breathing in gladness

Jane Upchurch

Inside

Outside
it is grey and cold
and blowy.
Inside I have lit candles,
it is golden and warm
and still.
This is an altar.
Here is a place
to find peace.

Lighting candles

Late Winter

It is cold,
a late winter day.
Yesterday the sun shone
and the daffodils beamed yellow.
You could feel spring coming near.

But it's not here today
so I've lit a fire.
Soon the season for them
will have gone.

I am not regretting
the absence of spring,
I am enjoying
the last of winter,
warmed by the fire.

Not regretting

Jane Upchurch

The Last Day of Winter

I am in the garden, often abandoned during the cold months of grey. It has been frosty overnight but now it is beginning warm, the sky a clear, sailing blue and the sun shining on us, on me.

The water feature is happy, it is gurgling. The birds are celebrating, they are singing. I close my eyes to the sun and I can feel its warmth fill the skin on my face and hold me. I am held by light.

Today is the last day of winter. Tomorrow is spring and I am alive in it, I am here and ready. I am shell and shore to its tide.

Closing my eyes to the sun

Pieces

Spring is Beginning to Show	6	Horse Chestnut Trees	35
The End of Dawn	7	The Gravel Garden	36
Spring Sings	8	Peony	37
Bless the Rain	9	Shining	38
Perfume	10	Another Day	39
Humble Hands	11	Blessing	40
Jenny	12	Soaking in the Rain	41
At the Bottom of my Garden	13	Walking my Dog	42
Surprises	14	Refuge	43
Birch Leaf	15	Into the Garden	44
Random	16	Bruised	45
To Be Here	17	Blackberries	46
Holiday	18	Help	47
Skin	19	Windy	48
A Meditation	20	Dorset	49
Days Aren't Always Sunny	21	Sitting	50
Buddleia	22	An Ordinary Life	51
Primroses	23	Roses	52
Silence	24	Obligations	53
Replace the Chaos	25	Perfection	54
Blossom	26	The Chaos and the Splendour	55
The Magic of Forgiveness	27	Lawns	56
Day and Night	28	Five Course Meal	57
Oak	29	My Rule	58
Spring	30	Scars	59
Mirrors	31	Prayer	60
Longing	32	Solstice	61
The Ground is a Bed	33	Summer Sun	62
May	34	Lichen	63

Shelling Peas	64	Evening	96
Fullness	65	Moonlight	97
My Rock	66	Smelling Autumn	98
Bless You	67	Choreography	99
With Arms Out	68	Gentle	100
Blue Geraniums	69	Starlings	101
Driving Slowly	70	A Call	102
Walking the Grass	71	Encounter	103
No Words	72	Twilight in November	104
Showers	73	Grey	105
The Present	74	Dusk	106
Sunday Morning	75	Autumn Leaves	107
Friends	76	The Sun is a Moon	108
Day Prayer	77	Fired with Light	109
Tired	78	Winter Solstice	110
Hibiscus	79	Window	111
Beauty	80	Lemon	112
The Gift of Spirit	81	A Winter's Day	113
Lizard	82	This Day	114
Selfish	83	The Shelter of Dark	115
The Adaptability of Love	84	Snowlight	116
Getting Up First	85	Secret Snow	117
God of the Garden	86	February	118
Hawthorn	87	Little Things	119
Sunshine in my Soul	88	Lavender	120
Rambling Rose	89	Inside	121
Sky	90	Late Winter	122
The Code	91	The Last Day of Winter	123
Walking	92	Pieces	124
Rays of Light	93		
Green Glass	94		
The Last Day of Summer	95		

Also by the Author

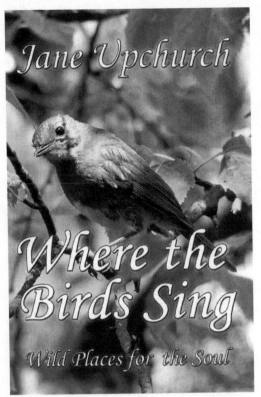

Where the Birds Sing

There is a magic quality to wild places that restores the soul. They feed a need deep inside us for something beyond what we have created, something bigger than us, something untamed that can pry loose the knots in our psyche and blow away the dust. Most of us don't live near places of uninterrupted wild. We have to make do with the pockets that patchwork our domain. And they are there if we look, if we notice. They are where the birds sing.

The ultimate in experiencing the wild is God. In the developed world God too has been cut out - or tamed to fit in. But just like wind-blown seeds, the Spirit has ways of finding our cracks and crevasses and making them green.

In this book Jane responds to the wild places she encounters - in the countryside, the weather, her garden, her God. Perhaps the pieces she has written will help you to discover wild places of your own.

Order your copy now!

www.onwardsandupwards.org/products/where-birds-sing